Healing
In the
Midst of Brokenness

Healing
In the
Midst of Brokenness

A Practical Guide to
Pastoral Care in Times of Crises

Dr. Carolyn V. Hodge

I AM The Living Word Ministries, Inc.
Bowie, Maryland

Healing in the Midst of Brokenness
Copyright © 2017 by I AM The Living Word Ministries, Inc.

Scripture quotations in this book are taken from the King James Version of the Bible, unless otherwise noted in the text. Scripture quotations marked AMP are taken from the Amplified Version of the Bible. Scripture quotations marked NAS are taken from the New American Standard Version of the Bible. The following Bible translation was used: The Comparative Study Bible, copyright ©1984 by The Zondervan Bible Publishers.

All rights reserved under International Copyright Law. No part of this book may be reproduced or transmitted in any form or by any means without written permission of the Publisher, except for the inclusion of brief quotations in a review.

Cover design by TLH Designs, www.tlhdesigns.com
Interior layout and design by Kingdom Living Publishing,
　　www.kingdomlivingbooks.com

For information about this book or to contact the author, write to:
I AM The Living Word Ministries, Inc.
3450 Crain Highway, Suite 231
Bowie, Maryland 20716

Published by:

I AM The Living Word Ministries, Inc.
3450 Crain Highway, Suite 231
Bowie, Maryland 20716

Published in the United States of America.

ISBN 978-0-692-71953-4

Table of Content

1. Introduction — 7
2. Dualism Concerning Healing and Wholeness — 13
3. Healing Viewed and Defined
   By Theologians and Scholars — 21
4. Favorable View on Healing and Wholeness — 33
5. Theological Implications
   On Healing and Wholeness — 37
6. Ministering Healing and Wholeness to the Dying — 65
7. Ministering Healing and Wholeness
   To Those Who Experience Spousal Abuse — 85
8. Conclusion — 99

Chapter 1

Introduction

There are people in today's world who are suffering with many types of hurts in their lives. Some of these hurts are either physical, psychological, or spiritual or a combination of two or more of these entities. A few of these hurts can be the result of deeply rooted issues or may have been brought on as a result of some traumatic experience or experiences in the individual's life. As ministers, I believe that we have an obligation to be available to assist people through such difficult times. Further, I believe that our assistance should not be limited to just the members of our congregation, but should include those within our communities and our own personal loved ones.

A case in point: Carrie Blake, my mother, was diagnosed with cancer of the breast at age 69. After a lumpectomy, radiation, and chemotherapy, the cancer went into remission. By the age of 74, however, the cancer had reoccurred. This time it had spread throughout her body and was attacking her vital organs—her lung and stomach. Her physicians had advised her that additional chemotherapy might be able slow the progression of this illness. She refused to undergo any additional chemotherapy. I believe that this refusal was because prior chemotherapy had caused her to become gravely ill. Previously, she had experienced extraordinary bouts with nausea and extreme tiredness, extreme weakness, loss of taste—nothing seemed good to her physical body during this period of extreme, debilitating hurt, physical brokenness, and, perhaps, even emotional brokenness (which I believe she hid from her family quite well).

Another case in point: A young woman has been married for just over two years. She finds that her marriage is falling apart. She has discovered that her spouse is not the individual that he had portrayed himself to be while they were dating. This young woman had met her spouse in a church. He had been a member of the church for just over a year when they met. They started dating and attending Bible Study together each week. They participated in multiple church activities. He even sang in the Men's Choir and the Mass Choir.

As she attempted to get to know her boyfriend/fiancée even greater over the first two years prior to their wedding, she had asked him many questions about his character, his past practices, and his lifestyle prior to becoming a church member. He had told her that he used to be a drinker—"just a couple of beers"—before becoming a Christian. In addition, he had told her that he had dabbled in drugs, but that there was nothing really serious in this. He stated that he had given all of that up when he became a Christian. He explained that he was a new person in Jesus.

After a year and a half of marriage, she noticed that her spouse had started coming home late with the smell of alcohol on his breath. He had told her that he was just hanging out with a few office friends. Also, he started telling her that he had to work late and on weekends at the office. This occurred quite often. Ultimately, she discovered by reviewing a cell phone bill that her spouse had been making telephone calls to a particular number at various times late at night or very early in the morning. She discovered that the calls were going to another woman. Upon confronting him about this situation, he claimed that he was counseling her—that she was going through a difficult time in her marriage and he was attempting to help her through this process. This story did not hold up, because later, he stated that it was because he was going through a difficult time in his marriage and the woman was providing counseling to him. It had become obvious to this young woman that her spouse had been cheating on her and that the late office and weekend hours were in reality a time for rendezvous with a female member of his office. As she queried him about this, he became increasingly more hostile, which eventually erupted into verbal abuse and physical altercations. These experiences were very psychologically and spiritually traumatic to this young woman. She became bewildered at how she possibly could cope with such emotional turmoil and hurt in the midst of marital brokenness—broken covenant, broken vows, broken commitments, broken trust, and a broken heart.

When an individual is hurting, it seems natural to want to ease their pain and suffering. The questions become "How do we help to heal the brokenness that looms before them? Where do we begin? What do we say to them? What resources are available to us that we can provide to them during such times of physical, psychological, and spiritual crises? What have theologians and biblical scholars said about similar situations of seeming hopelessness? What do the Scriptures say about such situations? How did they address the whole notion of healing and wholeness?

These two cases are presented herewith as teaching experiences to assist ministers and parishioners in similar circumstances. This book will address the topic of "healing and wholeness in the midst of brokenness" and answer the questions noted above and provide some practical guidance to ministers as they work to provide healing and wholeness to individuals, who are going through very difficult, stressful, and traumatic times in their lives. This book will begin this process by taking a look at healing and wholeness as defined in the Scriptures, by looking at the positions of the great philosophical thinkers on the subject of healing and by assessing the theological implications on this topic of healing and wholeness, by attempting to address each of the above questions (not necessarily in the order presented above), and by presenting recommendations for ministering to the needs of the individuals identified in the above two cases. By presenting recommendations regarding these two scenarios, it is my hope that others, who may be going through such trials and those who are ministering to such individuals, may be blessed, delivered, healed, and set free from their bondages—their circumstances of brokenness and experience healing in the midst of brokenness.

Chapter 2

Dualism Concerning Healing and Wholeness

Since the beginning of the twentieth century, there has been renewed interest in spiritual healing and wholeness. In 1906, reportedly there was a great outpouring of the Holy Spirit upon a small group of people on Azusa Street in California.[1] According to the reports, many people were healed of varied illnesses and diseases, including mental and physical illnesses. Those who were the recipient of such healings attributed their healing experiences to a great move and the miracles of God. Among those who professed their experiences and believed that their accounts of healing were a move of God were those who were skeptical of such occurrences.

This duplex view appears in today's society as it did almost one hundred years ago. Yet, during this span of time, many people have claimed to experience miraculous healings. In order to understand why there is such a dichotomy of understandings concerning these phenomena, we must begin to look at how we have come to have such a wide variance concerning the notions of healing and wholeness. We will start by looking at the Scriptures and move on to look at the thoughts of the great thinkers, who have wrestled with the issues of healing and wholeness over time.

Healing and Wholeness

On the matter of healing, Matthew 12:15 notes, "Jesus ... *withdrew Himself from thence: and great multitudes followed Him, and He healed them all.*" Healing in this context is derived from a Greek word meaning in essence to attend to as in cherishing someone. Further, its meaning infers "to wait upon," "to relieve (of disease):

cure."² This Scripture show us that Jesus attended to the "great multitude," because He cherished them. Jesus waited upon them "to relieve" them of their diseases. He "cured" them.³

According to John 14:12, Jesus stated, "Verily, verily, I say unto you, he that believeth on Me; the works that I do shall he do also; and greater works than these shall he do; . . ." Thus, as ministers and followers of Jesus, the Christ, we are to do the works that Jesus has done. What were some of those works? Jesus answered in His own defense, when responding to John the Baptist's question of whether or not He was the expected Messiah. Jesus' response was, "The *blind receive their sight, and the lame walk, the lepers are cleansed, and deaf hear, the dead are raised up, and the poor have the gospel preached to them*" (Matthew 11:3-5). Not only did Jesus do these things, but Jesus also "*cast out the spirits...*" (Matthew 8:16 NAS). This refers to those persons who were "demon-possessed." According to this Scripture, "*When evening had come, they brought to Him many who were demon-possessed; and He cast out the spirits with a word, healed all who were ill.*"

On the matter of wholeness, John 5:2-9 states,

"Now there is at Jerusalem by the sheep market a pool, which is called in Hebrew tongue Bethesda, having five porches. In these lay a great multitude of impotent folk, of blind, halt, withered, waiting for the moving of the water. For an angel went down at a certain season into the pool, and troubled the water: whosoever then first after the troubling of the water stepped in was made whole of whatsoever disease he had. And a certain man was there, which had an infirmity thirty and eight years. When Jesus saw him lie, and knew that he had been now a long time in that case, He saith unto him, Wilt thou be made whole? The impotent man answered him, Sir, I have no man, when the water is troubled, to put me into the pool: but while I am coming, another steppeth down before me. Jesus saith unto him, Rise, take up thy bed, and walk. And immediately the man was made whole, and took up his bed, and walked."

John 7:13 states, "... *I have made a man every whit whole on the Sabbath day.*" In this context, the above noted Scripture refers to the Greek translation for "whole." In this instance, "whole" means being made "healthy; i.e., well (in body)."[4]

> "*And, behold, a woman, which was diseased with an issue of blood twelve years, came behind him, and touched the hem of his garment: For she said within herself, If I may but touch His garment, I shall be whole. But Jesus turned Him about, and when He saw her, He said, Daughter, be of good comfort; thy faith hath made thee whole. And the woman was made whole from that hour*" (Matthew 9:20-22).

In this Scripture, the Greek word for "whole" means "to save; i.e., deliver or protect ... heal, preserve, save (self), do well, be (make) whole."[5] In this context, Jesus delivered the woman from a twelve-year long infirmity. Not only was she delivered, she was protected from having to go through this physical ordeal any further, not to mention any ridicule that she may have experienced as a result of her infirmity. Jesus had delivered and saved her from all of this. She was made "whole" from the infirmity. She was made "whole" from the ridicule of those within her community, because of the infirmity. She was made "whole" from any future need to visit physicians concerning this ailment. She was made "whole"—delivered, protected, healed, preserved, and saved to do well from this point on. This Scripture supports the notions that the woman was not only cured of her illness, she was "delivered" (set free) from everything that was associated with this infirmity—ridicule (perhaps even a shunning from family, friends, and acquaintances) associated with being ill. Perhaps she would begin to experience some notoriety because of having experienced this healing (cure). This could have a positive impact upon her self-esteem, her position within her family and community.

The above noted Scriptures confirm healing and wholeness as a result of the spoken word. In these Scriptures, Jesus spoke to the situation or to the person's faith in Him and the result was a healing—a cure, and/ or wholeness. The New Testament is full of healing and wholeness stories as a result of Jesus' ministry. Not only does the New Testament speak of Jesus' ministry in this arena, it speaks of Jesus' followers, who were able to perform similar miracles of healing and wholeness by invoking the name of Jesus. The following Scriptural story is a case in point:

"Now Peter and John went up together into the temple at the hour of prayer, being the ninth hour. And a certain man lame from his mother's womb was carried, whom they laid daily at the gate of the temple which is called Beautiful, to ask alms of them that entered into the temple. Who seeing Peter and John about to go into the temple asked an alms. And Peter, fastening his eyes upon him, said, Look on us. And he gave heed unto them, expecting to receive something of them. Then Peter said, Silver and gold have I none; but such as I have give I thee: In the name of Jesus Christ of

Nazareth rise up and walk. And he took him by the right hand, and lifted him up: and immediately his feet and ankle bones received strength. And he leaping up stood, walked, and entered with them into the temple, walking, and leaping, and praising God" (Acts 3:1-8).

Thus, we see that Peter and John, disciples and followers of Jesus, believed that they could do the "greater works" that Jesus had told them that they could do prior to Jesus' death, burial, and resurrection. Jesus had stated that if anyone believed on Him, "The *works that (He did) that shall he (she) do also; and greater works than these shall he do..."* (John 14:12).

Now, the question becomes, "How did Jesus' followers get to the point that ministering gifts of healing and wholeness are no longer applicable to ministry, today?" Looking at the views of modern theologians and scholars may give us some clues.

Chapter 3

Healing Viewed and Defined By Theologians and Scholars

According to Morton Kelsey, "modern Christian churches believe that they have nothing directly to do with healing the sick. They do not think that the church's action—its religious acts—have any direct effect on human health."[1] He observes that "religious groups do build hospitals and medical centers, but this does not differ from any other act of charity or compassion. In fact, it has come to be widely believed that there is no particular relation between the practice of Christianity and sound health of mind and body."[2] This position on healing is diametrically opposed to what Jesus taught His disciples and His followers. How did Christian churches get to this point in their belief systems?

Kelsey has presented four views of healing that exist in the modern Protestant church. One view is that "our bodies can be cared for adequately by medical and physical means alone and that religious help is superfluous." Since the early 1900s, it has appeared that modern medicine would be able to eliminate all communicable diseases. Deaths as a result of such diseases as gastritis, tuberculosis, and influenza and pneumonia have decreased considerably. Thus, the belief that modern medicine, with the best possible research, would be able to eliminate all diseases. The result in the church has been to ignore and rationalize certain portions of the Christian messages. The portions of the Christian messages that have been eliminated included "the healings done by Jesus and His followers (which alone account for a fifth of the narrative portions of the gospels), the outpouring of the Holy Spirit along with other strange phenomena at Pentecost and in apostolic times, the dreams and visions, the references to angelic and evil spirits in the New

Testament, indeed the whole emphasis on the interrelation of body, soul, and spirit."[3]

The second view is that sickness is a direct "disciplinary gift" from God. The sickness thereby serves as an opportunity to become reconnected to God through prayer, reading the Scriptures, and meditating on the Scriptures. It is expected that going through the sickness will add to and strengthen ones faith. In this instance, sickness is viewed as a visitation from God.[4] Thus, sickness is viewed as something that one should endure with patience while allowing God to perform His perfect work in that individual. In the sixteenth century when an individual became ill, it was expected that that individual or a member of that individual's family would notify the Minister of the Parish. The minister would visit the sick person and pray for him or her. The prayer would be taken from the English Book of Common Prayer for this purpose. It is still in this source, today, in England.[5] Also, it was a part of the Episcopal Church in America until 1928. Note below a portion of the prayer that was delivered to a sick individual.

> "... Sanctify, we beseech thee, this thy fatherly correction to him; that the sense of his weakness may add strength to his faith, and seriousness to his repentance. That, if it shall be thy good pleasure to restore him to his former health, he may lead the residue of his life in thy fear, and to thy glory: or else, give him grace so to take thy visitation that, after this painful life is ended, he may dwell with thee in life everlasting through Jesus Christ our Lord."[6]

Here we see that sickness is considered as a visitation from God, as a matter of discipline that is to be endured until the sick person fully repented for whatever wrong he had done. In keeping with this line of reasoning, a special prayer book for the sick was developed for this purpose. Even though the minister may have asked for God's mercy in a particular situation, this appears to depict God as merciless and vengeful, particularly if the ill person was ill due to no fault of his/her own.

The third view is known as "dispensationalism." Dr. Wade Boggs, a fundamentalist, is a proponent of this view. Dispensationalism has to do with the belief that God originally gave certain gifts to the church, including the gift of healing, to "get the church established." Thus, it appears that dispensationalism applied only to the first few centuries of the early church. Once the church was fully established worldwide, there was no longer a need for such gifts to operate within the church.[7] Martin Luther and John Calvin supported this view. Luther believed that the real gift of the Holy Spirit was to enlighten humankind, not to dispense or exercise gifts, such as raising the dead and healing. Calvin stated that the "gifts of healing disappeared with the other miraculous powers which the Lord was pleased to give for a time ...."[8] Karl Barth neither denied nor affirmed the gift of healing for today. "Healing was dismissed by neglect rather than by denial."[9] In Barth's commentary, the *Epistle to the Romans*, he did not mention any of the signs and wonders spoken of by Paul in his writing (Chapter 15, verses 18-19).

The fourth view is that of "rational materialism and existentialism." This is the "theology of Bultmann," which expresses the idea that "there is no supernatural agency which can break into the autonomous physical worlds ruled by natural law. Since Bultmann and those who go along with him are in theological ascendancy at present, this all adds up to a very strong case against spiritual healing."[10] Bultmann viewed "the gospel accounts of healing as 'mythology.'" Thus, all references to the miraculous, as cited in the Bible, are rejected. Included in this line of thought are Kiekegaard and Nietzsche to whom "many religious philosophers have turned in the effort to find some reasonable base for Christian faith in the sophisticated modern world."[11]

Two schools of thought have emerged—Christian existentialism and the "God is dead" movement. In each instance, a position is taken that is completely against the notion of Christian healing.[12] Existentialism affirms that, "Nothing is real but the present moment of existence." It "discards any idea of supernatural nonphysical reality existing apart from personal psychic material. It questions the value of history, and accepts as axiomatic a scientific understanding of the world a closed and inevitably physical system. The course of nature cannot be broken into or interrupted by any powers beyond "existence;" instead meaning comes to human beings as they authentically live in this immediate, conscious situation. They then discover the ground of their being."[13] According to Kierkegaard, the supernatural was "irrelevant in Christian thought" and saw no value in the history of Jesus.[14] From this line of reasoning, the "God is dead" movement emerged. This thought became a logical conclusion based upon the presentations of the "great" thinkers of their day. Thus, it appears that both the Catholic and Protestant faiths have been "swept clean of any idea of Christian healing."[15] Consequently, the Christian church has focused on material things in the world; i.e., building hospitals, constructing church buildings, raising money, political/social issues, and using business techniques to accomplish these tasks. Emphasis has been in the size of the congregation, the number and variety of programs that can be provided in the church, and the physical needs—food, clothing, shelter—of church members, rather than on the spiritual needs of the individuals within the congregation.

Considering the above four views that have impacted the belief systems of the Christian church (which was established on the foundations of Jesus, the Christ), one cannot help but wonder "how it is possible to take the ethical and moral teachings of Jesus seriously when nearly half the verses in the New Testament" have been ignored and/or avoided, such as the gift of healing, due to the intrusion of these "modern" ideas and views—existentialism, dispensationalism, modern medicine as a cure-all, and a vengeful God, who metes out sickness.[16]

As a member of the Pentecostal faith, I disagree with the negative views of Christian healing. I believe that from the foundation of the Christian church up to this day, the gifts of the Holy Spirit to the Christian church are still available for the Christian believers. These gifts of the Holy Spirit include the word of wisdom, the word of knowledge, faith, healing, working of miracles, prophecy, discerning of spirits, divers kinds of tongues, and interpretation of tongues. These gifts come by way of "the *manifestation of the Spirit, which is given to every man to profit withal ..., dividing to every man severally as He will*" (1 Corinthian 12:7-11).

The human mind does not appear to be able to fully comprehend God's unsearchable greatness (Psalm

145:3), and because of this many of us are unwilling to dare to trust God and fully believe God's Word. The Apostle Paul reveals that his assignment was to *"preach among the Gentiles the unsearchable riches of Christ; and to make all men see what is the fellowship of the mystery, which from the beginning of the world hath been hid in God, who created all things by Jesus Christ…"* (Ephesians 3:8). Paul goes on to tell us that we should not be ignorant about God's spiritual gifts (the special endowments of supernatural energy) (1 Corinthians 12:1 AMP) God appears to be willing to share with us His great mysteries, particularly in the realm of spiritual gifts. However, it appears that there is a definite caveat—fellowship with God—necessary to attain prior to the manifestation of spiritual gifts. Deuteronomy tells us that if we seek the Lord God with all of our heart and with all our soul, then we shall find God (Deuteronomy 4:29). Strong's Concordance tells us that the word, seek, means in Hebrew "to search out (by any method, specifically in worship or prayer)." The second meaning of seeks infers "to tread or frequent." This implication appears to mean that one must fellowship with God often in worship and in prayer, and then one should be able to establish a relationship with God. Once the relationship is established, then God will give "the manifestation of the Spirit" to the one who fully searches for God—to learn God's ways. "Manifestation" in this context comes from the Greek word "exhibition; i.e., (figuratively) expression … [a] bestowment …."[17] Thus, it is incumbent upon us to diligently seek God and to learn His ways. Then, according to God's will, He will "express" His self through the "exhibition" of His gifts as He "chooses" (1 Corinthians 12:7-11). Healing and wholeness are among the gifts of God that He seeks to reveal to humanity, particularly to those who diligently seek Him—routinely worship and pray often and spend time meditating upon His Word.

Not all scholars have the view of the scholars presented above. Their view appears to be strictly secular in nature. There are some scholars who have researched the topic of healing and wholeness and have a favorable view towards this topic. For example, George Mallone tells us, "It is possible for all the gifts of the Holy Spirit to function in the church today."[18] He goes on to say that "[no] where in Scripture does it say that gifts of the Spirit have ceased. Scripture teaches us to stir up and exercise these gifts and how to test their validity. But only when Jesus Christ comes again are we to expect their cessation."[19]

The next chapter of this book will present additional favorable viewpoints.

Chapter 4

Favorable Views
On Healing and Wholeness

Dr. R. A. Lambourne once offered this definition of healing, 'Healing is a satisfactory response to a crisis, made by a group of people, both individually and corporately.' This was quoted by Michael Wilson who then supplemented it by explaining the 'satisfactory response' as 'restoration to purposeful living in society'.[1]

I like what Morris Maddocks says about healing in his book, *The Christian Healing Ministry*. Maddocks defines healing as "the process which brings about the restoration to health." He goes on to say that healing has to do with "spaciousness and growth."[2] He says that this spaciousness and growth harks "back to the unleashing of the explosive force inherent in the act of creation, a power in nature that can even use suffering for an eventual good and takes setbacks into its evolutionary process."[3] Maddocks notes that when it comes to healing, we humans routinely consider only physical healing. Yet the purpose of the Creator is much greater than we can imagine. Just as we have seen with the woman with the issue of blood, Jesus not only healed her physical ailment, He made her whole—in spirit, in soul (her mind, will, and emotions), as well as in her physical body.

In addition to Maddocks' position on healing, Bruce Epperly reminds us, "As followers of Jesus, we are called to embody the healing work of God. We are called to affirm our partnership with God by challenging illness wherever it is found, regardless of its causes."[4] Healing and wholeness from this author's perspective deals with not only the cure of a physical condition, but would include the wholeness issues; e.g., "finding alternatives to the violence in the media and in the streets" and involving oneself in the political arenas that impact the social ills of society, such as cultural/social discrimination, health care for the poor, job opportunities for the disenfranchised and the marginalized in society. "While the light of God's power is at work in our lives and the lives of others, we must work to heal the sick and welcome the outcast...." Our charge as Ministers is to "[c]are for those who are not whole...."[5] We are to "relieve suffering and effect cures of body, mind, and spirit."[6] We are to minister healing and wholeness.

Jesus told His followers that they were to do the "works" that He had done. He went on to say that His followers should do even "greater works." Jesus has expected that His Church, the Body of Christ, to take up the call to do "greater works." After Jesus' death, burial, resurrection, and ascension, according to the book of Acts, many of the followers of Jesus, the Christ, did the "works" of Jesus. These works continued throughout the first three centuries of the early church. Further, over a period of centuries, since the start of the early church, there have been spurts of phenomenal moves of God in the area of healing and wholeness.

The next chapter of this book will present some miraculous moves of God that began in the early 1900s.

Chapter 5

Theological Implications

On Healing and Wholeness

Prior to his death in 1925, Frank Bartleman, who was greatly impacted by the revival in Wales in the early 1900s and the revival that burst forth on Azusa Street in California in 1906, delivered the message provided below. During this time, there were demonstrations of the miraculous, including the nine gifts of the Spirit quoted in 1 Corinthians 12:7-11. I believe that this message is worth repeating to the churches of our day. We need to be revived and empowered by the Spirit of Christ, as the Body of Christ, in order to minister to the needs of the people, who live in the world today.

The world is the field; the true church is treasure—like a kernel in a shell. But the great nominal church, the ecclesiastical body in each generation, is also like a field in which the true spiritual church—living church—like a treasure, is hidden.

But even if this is true, the spiritual church is far from being the treasure of divine life and power originally planned and provided for in the purpose of God. Ever since the early church fell from New Testament purity and life, she has been like a backslider, fallen from the summit of apostolic day—though destined to return and yet enter into the full blessing of the Father's house.

I refer to the true, spiritual body of Christ. It is a prodigal son, wandered from the Father's house, but since the Reformation gradually returning. Nearly five centuries have now passed since the Reformation. The route back has been devious and long, with many a dark valley, as well as many a glorious summit. But steadily, relentlessly, the mighty Spirit of God has been moving on, restoring that which was lost adding things up toward that great prophetic revelation of the body of Christ in unity and fullness—even one body, fully matured *"unto the measure of the stature of the fullness of Christ"* (Ephesians 4:13).

Beloved, unless we understand this, we will not be able to move on with God and understand the different stages, experiences, and various standards and operations in the church's history during this dispensation. That is why most Christians have failed to move on with God and to accept His cumulative unfoldings in the restoration of revelation, light, and experience, once lost, but now being rested to the true church.

If you do not fully see this, if it seems to differ from your present idea of things, do bear with me. Before I am finished, I believe you will understand; and, if so, it may well transform your life, giving new and vital direction to your prayers and ministry.

The Heart of Our Trouble

The human soul is very lazy toward God, and one generation has seemed to be able to travel very far on its way back to God and His standard from which the early church fell. It is true that human error or understanding continually satisfies itself with a part instead of the whole, but the real fact is that men are not willing to pay full price to get back fully to God's standard, to be all the Lord's.

The early church came forth from the Upper Room fresh in her "first love" (Revelation 2:4), baptized with the Holy Spirit, filled with God, possessing both the graces and fruits of the Spirit, and with a 100 percent consecration for God. This was the secret of her power. She was all for God, and God was all for her. This principle will apply in all ages, both individually and collectively. No sacrifice on the altar means no fire. The fire of God never falls on an empty altar. The greater the sacrifice, the more the fire.

When the prodigal gets home, and the church becomes 100 percent for God again, we will have the same power, the same life – and the same persecution from the world. The reason we have so little persecution now is that the Spirit cannot press the claims of God home on the world through us. When that happens, men must either surrender or fight.

"Jesus Christ, the same yesterday, and today, and forever" (Hebrews 13:8)! God never changes. We have changed. We are not waiting for God. God is waiting for us. The Holy Spirit is given; we are still in the dispensation opened on the Day of Pentecost. But God can only work when we are willing, yielded, and obedient. We tie God's hands.

The history of the church has been the same. Each company that has come forth in the line of restoration has run the same course. That is human, fallen nature. It is human failure, not God's. When everything dries up and dies out, we call upon God. This alone makes it possible for God to come. He must have some place to put His Spirit, and only empty vessels can be filled.

When we are filled with our own ways, think ourselves *"rich, and increased with good"* spiritually (Revelation 3:17), God can give us nothing. *"To the hungry soul every bitter thing is sweet"* (Proverbs 27:7). The crumbs tasted good to the Syrophoenician woman, but well-fed children despise even dainties. (See Matthew 15:21-28.) They will throw the food across the table at one another. Like the children of Israel, they despise even *"angels' food"* (Psalm 78:23).

The best preacher in the land cannot preach with liberty when his message is not desired or received. The oil ceases to flow as soon as there are no more empty vessels to be filled. This will often explain why good preachers sometimes have liberty and at other times have no anointing. Criticism will stop the flow of oil through any preacher. Oil will not flow when frozen.

Theological Implications

How It All Began

The early church ran well for a season. Everything went down before it. But by the third or fourth century, they had compromised to escape the cross. They sold out to the Devil, backslid, and went down into the Dark Ages. They lost the Holy Spirit anointing, the gifts, the life, the power, the joy, everything. The church became a prodigal, left the Father's house, and went to feeding swine.

The Devil found he could not stamp out the early church by killing them. For every one he killed, two sprang up. Like the children of Israel, *"the more they afflicted thee, the more they multiplied and grew"* (Exodus 1:12). The early Christians vied with one another for a martyr's crown. They exposed themselves purposely, recklessly, for this reward. Someone has said the greatest call that ever came to man is the call to suffer. It is a noble cause.

Heaven was real to the early church—far more real than earth. In fact, they seem to have lived only for the next age. That was their longing, their goal, to be delivered from *"this present evil world"* (Galatians 1:4). It was the sole relief to which they looked forward. This present life, after all, is the true saint's purgatory. It is the sinner's heaven—his only heaven—and that is sad beyond words to express! But, glory to God, it is our only hell! We are in the Enemy's country, running the gauntlet, with foes lined up on all sides—but we're just passing through.

Without question, it was God's desire to restore the backslidden, prodigal church at once, when she fell, just as He must have desired at once to restore the human race in the beginning, when they fell. But He could not. Human, fallen nature was too weak.

God also wanted to take the children of Israel right into Canaan from Kadesh-Barnea when He brought them out of Egypt. It was only a short journey, but they frustrated His purpose and desire. They grieved God and *"limited the Holy One of Israel"* (Psalm 78:41), just as it has ever been. In

Theological Implications

consequence, they stopped going forward, went to "milling *around*," and their "carcasses *fell in the wilderness*" (Hebrews 3:17).

Beloved, whenever we stop going forward, we go to milling around. When an individual stops going forward for God, he begins to go in a circle, just as a man when lost in a forest ceases to go straightforward but wanders in a circle.

So it is with the early church. When they ceased to go forward, they started wandering in a circle and became lost in the Dark Ages. The Devil had found he could not destroy them or stop their march by persecuting and killing them; so he removed the cross, offering them titles, positions, honor, salaries, profits of every kind—and they fell for it.

They no longer needed to look to God for their protection and support. They were "like the nations round about them," just as the children of Israel when they rejected God as their King. (See Deuteronomy 17:14.) And so it is with our great church bodies of today. History repeats itself in every movement through human weakness and failure.

The Reformation and Subsequent History

Out of the Dark Ages came the great ecclesiastical, Roman hierarchy, which in time dominated the whole world, both political and religious. And the same condition has developed out of every fallen movement. An illegitimate, hybrid monster has come forth.

This was the condition of the formal church in Martin Luther's time. However, the living seed of the true church had remained buried in this mass, even through those long, dark centuries. This seed now began to spring up and germinate—the church within the church. The prodigal backslider began to come to himself at last and desire to return home. The church had fed on swine long enough!

Through the labors of such men as Huss, Wycliffe, Luther, Foxe, Wesley, Darby, Muller,

Moody, Evan Roberts, Wigglesworth, and a host of others, the prodigal church has been coming home. But each company that God has been able to bring forth and give a fresh deposit of the Spirit and of the truth once lost has sooner or later stopped short of the full goal. Although often gaining much ground and experiencing tremendous blessing, each group has ceased to go forward as a body and completely return to the early New Testament standard realization.

Again and again the church climbed from the depths of some sectarian stranglehold, with its various stages of formalism and spiritual darkness, only to fall again, within perhaps only a generation, into sometimes an even worse state. Fortunately, each time, some new light and understanding of truth and God's ways were given upon which the next revival company have broken fellowship, divided the children of God, and put the church in bondage to men and their ideas, standards, understandings, and opinions.

We must keep moving! The clearest light on truth and experience has not yet come. We still wait for the full restoration of the "pattern shown in the mount," that of the early New Testament apostolic church as a whole.

The great mistake has been to stop with sectarian, partial, abnormal revelations. We must keep our eyes on God, not on a party. Keep free from a party spirit. That is indicative of a respect of persons. Seek only God and His plan as a whole, His church as a whole.

Every company, in time, repeats the experience of the early church. They compromise to escape the cross and accept positions, salaries, titles, and ecclesiastical power. An ecclesiastical hierarchy arises, just as it did in the early church during the second and third centuries.

The backslidden church is still in an abnormal condition. It will continue to be so until it becomes fully restored to the first standard of apostolic Christianity from which it fell. No experience or revelation in the line of gradual restoration has been perfect in itself. All is abnormal, both in understanding and experience, until the perfect whole is realized and restored.

We need a readjustment of all our doctrines to the full, clear light of God in the Word. All past experiences must be examined and redefined in the light of the perfect whole.

Someone has said that every reformation is at its best and highest tide when it first comes forth. This would seem to be so, but at the same time the true church is ever moving on to maturity. I speak of the church within the church, the kernel in the shell, not the surrounding movement. Just as the individual believer who goes on with God gradually matures, so the church within the church is maturing toward the end of the age when she will be a full-growth church. The goal is not just the standard lost by the early church but that toward which they themselves were pressing—"*a fully matured man,*" even "*the measure of the stature of the fullness of Christ*" (Ephesians 4:13).

Apostasy and Recovery

As with Israel in the Exodus, the "mixed multitude" (Exodus 12:38), the exterior shell of every movement with which it loads itself and in which it later becomes buried, falls to lusting or "flesh." One can usually judge the progress of this process by the things the movement comes to demand. Instead of delight in the pure Word, prayer, worship, a love for souls, and zeal for good works, there come entertainment, programs, musicals, sensationalism, and oratory. These things have no place in essential, true Christianity, but are professionalism—flesh! O God, deliver us from fleshly substitutes for the Spirit.

Most meetings can only be kept by continuous entertainment, professional evangelism, and a strong social spirit. And this is all too true in Pentecostal, Holiness, and interdenominational circles, as well as in the older denominations. Where is the Life itself that draw the people and bring God to them as in the beginning? This is not

New Testament. It is abnormal, grieving and limiting the Holy One of Israel in our midst.

Each movement seems to run its course faster than the one before it. Like the Niagara River, it flows downward more swiftly as it approaches the falls, the end of time. These are the last days of apostasy.

The fight gets harder as we get higher up in our restoration from the early church's fall. When Adam fell, the satanic powers intervened between the fallen race and God. God removed the seat of His presence with man from earth to heaven. So when the early church fell, she again lost the image of God that had, in a sense, been restored in New Testament days when the body of believers became the temple of the Holy Spirit. In a higher sense than Adam had known, the *"spiritual wickedness in high places"* (Ephesians 6:12) intervened between the church and God again. Now, the prodigal church, coming up out of the Dark Ages, has had to fight her way back through these evil powers. Each movement, as we go higher toward full restoration, has to meet a higher order of these wicked, spiritual powers and intelligences and hence must fight harder.

Each step forward necessarily requires a deeper preparation and greater spiritual equipment for a greater measure of restoration.

It was never God's decree that the experience of the church should be so long and drawn out in recovering the normal standard and going on to fullness. But we have ever sought to call our present abnormal understanding and experience normal. We must see that all has been abnormal since the early church's fall. Experiences, understanding—everything—has been partial, unbalanced, and abnormal. Nothing has been perfectly understood, and all the different truths and experiences have only been parts of the whole.

We have not understood these truths and experiences; just as no machine is properly and clearly understood in detail except as we understand the whole. We have been recovering the whole in parts, without seeing the whole – thus

Theological Implications

we so often distort and over-emphasize the truth or experience that our particular movement has recovered. I trust you grasp this, for it is very important.

The New Testament church in the book of Acts entered normally into the fullness of the Spirit immediately at its inception, as for instance at Cornelius' household in the tenth chapter of Acts. The different phases of our salvation were all viewed as just so many parts of one glorious, normal whole. But all the various movements in the restoration, since the early reformers, have ceased in their turn to go forward to full realization. They have established their party standard of a partial, abnormal revelation, putting a part for the whole. Then, in human vanity, they have each contended they had it all.

This is sectarianism, and it is like a lot of dams holding back God's people from flowing on toward the vast ocean of God's fullness. God cares little for these partial standards of men—their names, sects or parties, slogans or standards. All is only partial, distorted light that finally becomes the enemy of the real truth as the Lord marches on to glory.

Each oncoming wave of the sea toward high tide must fight its way through the last receding one. So it is with the different movements toward a final restoration of the church. The immediately preceding one especially hates and opposes the next oncoming one. What fools the Devil has made of us! Oh, that we might see it! However real and good, as far as they have gone, these past revivals and movements are each but faltering, uncertain steps toward the final goal.

Let's Go On!

God has but one church, whether in heaven where most of it is, or here on earth. And there is yet very much land to be possessed before we realize the divine purpose to which we are destined. We must recognize the whole body of Christ. In our human thoughts, we fail to recognize God when we meet Him. Those who dare to go further with God toward the full restoration are denounced and opposed by others as if they were of the Devil. And this was not just true of Luther and the Catholic Church, it was also true of Wesley and the Anglican Church, of Booth and the Methodist Church, and so on. And it is still true today. But, beloved, we must face it, the backslider has not yet been fully restored; the prodigal has not yet reached home. We must keep moving on!

Elijah's rain came out of clear sky, without even the sign of a cloud to begin with—the result of faith alone. So the Pentecostal outpouring came in 1906. And this has been the case with every revival. Revival is the property of faith, not sight. There is nothing for sight to see in fallen nature but hopelessness. Revival and restoration must come from God, out of a clear sky. We are earthly and fleshly, but God is Spirit. God's Word is spirit and life (John 6:63), and faith in that Word brings the living God on the scene regardless of circumstances or outward prospects.

Will God visit His people again? Why not? As surely as He has done it in the past, He will do it again. God's skies are full of Pentecosts. He only waits for us to claim them. Do we not need one? Then we can have it, when we are willing to pay the price of obedient faith.

The church is not fully restored. No past group, after it has waned, has had the faith and vision to move God to visit them again. If they had, they would not be strewn along the way as more or less dead movements, their bones bleaching in the wilderness. None of them had future faith. They stopped short of the goal. None of them went clear through. They *"limited the Holy One of Israel"* (Psalm 78:41), just as we do today. They would not pay the price. That was the trouble. But worse than this, they justified themselves in their abnormal standards opposed and condemned others who would go further. And still they do so.

The sin of the Jewish high church in Jesus' time was the same. They refused to go further themselves, and set themselves in their backslidden condition to oppose all who wished to go forward. That spelled their doom, and it will bring down the judgments of God on any denomination, movement, or group that follows in their steps.

But a Gideon's band is forming again today. Faith is rising. Another visitation from God is coming. It is only the Gideon's band that can ever bring or receive it—only a praying, consecrated, pilgrim band. They of the "mixed *multitude*" (Exodus 12:38) will not be in it, for they are too many and too fleshly. *"Upon man's flesh,"* the Lord said of the precious anointing oil in the tabernacle, *"shall it not be poured"* (Exodus 30:32). God usually has to work with the little things, the weak things—the small, consecrated groups.

"I will pour water upon him that is thirsty, and floods upon the dry ground" (Isaiah 44:3). Dryness is a condition that invites rain. At such times men cry for rain. It is a cause for encouragement when we thirst for God. *"Blessed are they which do hunger and thirst after righteousness: for they shall be filled"* (Matthew 5:6). It was after an awful drought

that Elijah's rain came. The rain is ready, beloved—when we want it, and when we are in a condition to receive it.

We must have the spirit of Caleb and Joshua, a different spirit from the multitude. They "wholly *followed the Lord*" (Numbers 32:12); therefore they entered Canaan with the next company to go forward. They had their portion in it, while the old crowd died in the wilderness. No movement, as a movement, has ever gone all the way through to full restoration for the reasons I have explained. Hence, we must never become the property of, or limit ourselves to, a party or a movement. **Worship only God. Join God in His great movement. Keep moving!** (Bold added for emphasis.)

The End Is Nearing

We are rounding the corner toward complete recovery. God is again pressing His full claims upon His church and upon the world in this, the end of the age. But the Devil is also pressing his claims with great vigor. Whom will we serve? It is either 100 percent for God or for the Devil—there is no neutral ground. We are nearing the awesome climax of this deadly war between the kingdom of God and the kingdom of Satan. Each must be at his best for his side.

A normal church is always 100 percent for God. There can be no flirting with the Enemy. The church has no other business than to carry the Gospel to the world and press the claims of God upon His own. All its energies and resources should be used with that one object in view. *"Then shall the end come"* (Matthew 24:14). God waits for this.

Nothing but the zeal and the 100 percent consecration of the early church, both in laboring for the salvation of the nations and in building up the one true worldwide church, will or can satisfy God. He will accept no substitutes or compromise with our ideas and fleshly plans. There simply must be an utter abandonment to His full will and His great eternal purpose in His own children! Nothing short of this can clear our conscience and responsibility on the day of judgment. We could have done this long ago, if we had willed to do so; but we have not. Oh, let us not delay longer, but at once go right up and storm the Enemy's citadels, vowing never to withdraw our sword until Jesus comes and the whole land is ours!

We are rapidly approaching the last days. I am convinced that God is going to put the church through the fire to destroy the dross. Judgment begins at the house of God (1 Peter 4:17). And, believe me, nothing but 100 percent reality will remain! A theoretical salvation will not do.

We are reaching the culmination of this age, and nothing but a practical application of the Gospel can hope to survive. All else will be destroyed by the fires of worldwide persecution. God can only defend obedience to His Word. Never fear—He is going to have a church without spot or wrinkle (Ephesians 5:27). But do you and I want to have a part in it? A sectarian, competitive, selfish, self-seeking church cannot survive. The church must return to the spirit of the early church in the book of Acts. She must yield to God and press into His "present *truth*" (2 Peter 1:12) for this late hour—or perish in the fires of persecution and in her own blood. *"Our God is a consuming fire"* (Hebrews 12:29)!

Let us go on![1]

In order to see God move in the realm of healing and wholeness, we need to consider and perhaps even heed the words of Frank Bartleman, a theologian who was able to touch the hem of God's presence. This yielded a great move of God among the people in the early 1900s that continues to impact the world, today—albeit in small pockets of society. As Bartleman stated, God uses the small things in a mighty way to confuse the so-called wise of this world.

I agree with Bartleman, that if we are to see a move of God in a great way, then we need to be fully committed to God and fully yielded to Him. As ministers of the gospel of Jesus, the Christ, we should establish a relationship with God. How does one do this? I believe that it is done through earnest praying and meditating on God and His Word. As we do these two major things, I believe God imparts His wisdom to us about His mysteries of His heavenly realms. I believe that as we seek to be in God's presence, He will "hear *from heaven*" (2 Chronicles 7:14) and respond to those of us, who earnestly seek Him. As we hear from God and seek His wisdom, He imparts it to us so that we in turn can pass on that which we have received from Him to those who are among our congregations. I believe that this is our responsibility as godly, ordained, and licensed ministers of the Gospel of Jesus Christ of Nazareth.

There appears to be two necessities for healing (cure) to take place—a miracle from God—for all cure is a miracle, whether it be by way of medicine or by way of a move of God; and the faith of the individual needing the cure. Scripture tells us that the woman with the twelve-year long illness was healed as a result of her touching the Lord's garment. The miracle was that "*virtue had gone out of Him*" (Mark 5:30). The "virtue" was the healing power of Jesus. Coupled with the miracle of healing (cure) was the faith of the one healed. This healing story tells us that Jesus said, *"Daughter, thy faith hath made thee whole ..."* (Mark 5:34).

We do not always understand why the miracle gift of healing (cure) does not always manifest itself. Paul Tillich, in his writing of *"The Relation of Religion and Health,"* has stated that there "is something in the structure of mind and reality which transcends itself, toward a special qualification of both the pre-rational and rational elements, namely the spiritual. ... All creations of the mind have such a spiritual element ...." Tillich goes on to say that "Spiritual healing is the depth-dimension of mental healing; it is potentially, if not actually, present, whether it expresses itself in the seriousness and profundity of the psychotherapeutic situation, or in explicitly religious manifestations."[2] If the cure does not occur, then perhaps it is something within the mind of the individual that does not allow the healing to occur. Perhaps it is the providence of God. Perhaps it is the faith level of the individual. Perhaps God has chosen an alternative to a cure. Perhaps God has chosen to provide "wholeness"—wholeness of the spirit, wholeness of the soul. We do not know why or why not healing (cure) does or does not occur, but this should not serve as a hindrance to our efforts as ministers to pray for healing (cure) should the individual request it. We should not doubt the power or the will of God to perform a miracle gift of healing. God is sovereign in this regardless of outcome.

At the beginning of this book, I presented two cases. One case dealt with the need to minister healing and wholeness to an individual who was dying of the ravages of cancer. The second case dealt with the need to minister healing and wholeness to an individual who was dealing with the suffering of going through a separation and ultimately a divorce. The next chapter of this book will focus on these two cases and will provide some suggestions for ministering to people going through such difficulties in their lives.

Chapter 6

Ministering Healing
And Wholeness to the Dying

Breast cancer is the leading cause of death among women ages 40-55, with approximately 175,000 new cases of invasive disease diagnosed and 44,000 deaths in 1999. Women who have a first-degree family member with the disease have a two-fold increase in risk compared to those without a family history; having two first-degree relatives increases the risk five-fold. Age also increases the risk, and nearly 80 percent of women cancer patients are over age 50 at the time of diagnosis. ... White women are slightly more likely to develop breast cancer than are African American women, but African American women are more likely to die from their cancer .... [1]

There are lifestyle risks that are factors for the development of breast cancer. Some of these factors include the use of oral contraceptives, receiving estrogen replacement therapy, having the first child after the age of 30, having no children, the consuming two to five alcoholic drinks daily, high fat diet, obesity, and the lack of physical exercise.

Regardless of the source or cause of cancer, it is a life-altering and jarring experience for the patient and the patient's family. For many people, religious beliefs and spirituality are important factors in how the patient and the family members of the patient cope with this difficult disease. I have often heard it said that it is not just one person, the patient, who is affected by cancer, but it is the patient's entire family that is impacted by this disease. As ministers, we will need to be prepared to minister to both the patient and the patient's family members. In addition, we will need to be prepared to provide grief counseling and bereavement care should the patient succumb to his or her illness.

As mentioned previously, Carrie Blake, my mother, died of breast cancer in 1996. Although it was difficult to watch her go through the ordeal associated with this disease, I learned how really strong a woman she was. She had always served as the matriarch of our family. Anyone could count on her to tell you the truth about life. She had a strong Christian background—AME Zion beginning at early childhood, Baptist upon relocating to Washington, D.C., and ultimately a converted Catholic for over thirty years of her remaining life. Her faith in God was strong. Although she was dying of cancer and had a desire to be cured, she had such a peace about her. After many years of battling this disease, she would often say, "Tomorrow isn't promised to anyone." I believe that she was fully trusting God to deliver her from this disease, by any means necessary, even if this meant death to this world. It was her faith that allowed her to go through this debilitating disease with her chin up and head held high until the end.

She never complained about her suffering. During her last days, she seemed to be completely at ease. The doctors and nurses made her as comfortable as possible. She was in and out of consciousness. She always had a smile on her face for her family members who came to visit her in the hospital. She was at peace with herself. She was at peace with her God. Just by observing her during this time, I felt as if she was still teaching us, as she did as we were growing up and on into our adult years. Now, she was teaching us how to die—to die with eloquence and with dignity. Mom trusted God. She trusted God to deliver her from her disease. She trusted God to deliver her from her pain. She trusted God to deliver her from suffering. She relied on the Scriptures. She read Bible-related materials. She even read books that were written by a Catholic priest, who had died of cancer. Her relationship with God, along with the Bible, and the additional reference materials served to comfort, console, and provide her with the wholeness that she needed in order to cope with her suffering. "Coping emerges out of the backdrop of cultural forces (Pargament, 1997)."[2] In mom's, her coping strategies emerged out of her cultural background as a result of her exposure when growing up in the AME Zion Church, as a young adult woman in the Baptist faith tradition, and as a mature and senior woman of the Catholic tradition. She was grounded in her faith.

What causes a person to be so strong at the final moments of his/her life? What causes others to be embittered in their final moments of life? How do we effectively minister to the family member of the dying? I can only expect that how one deals with the final moments of ones life has something to do with what Tillich expressed as spirituality—one's level of connectedness to God. It is a person's faith or the lack thereof that impacts how they go through suffering in this life, whether physical suffering or mental suffering or a combination thereof. In my mother's case she had a strong faith. Her life reflected this, even unto the end of her days.

How do we as church leaders effectively minister to the people of faith and those who have little to no faith? What do we do when "cure" does not happen? To be sure we need to have a personal relationship with our God—be strong worshippers and prayers. We need to pray for God's wisdom in each situation. No two situations concerning death and dying are exactly the same. To those of us who are called to minister to the sick the following is offered:

> Always treat each person as an individual. Find out their fears, misunderstandings, areas of belief and unbelief. Be ready to teach and to challenge as well as to comfort.[3]

This reference was found in the writing of D. S. Latimer, who recommends the use of "The Visitation of the Sick" found in *The Book of Common Prayer*. As we have seen earlier, this referenced source is used by the Church of England and has been in use since 1662. Those of us who are affiliated with this faith system may find this useful. However, for those of us not affiliated with this faith system, there are alternative ways for ministering to the sick:

> *Are any among you sick? They should call for the elders of the church and have them pray over them, anointing them with oil in the name of the*

Lord. The prayer of faith will save the sick, and the Lord will raise them up ... (James 5:13-15).

We must keep in mind that it is not faith that heals, "although faith is present when healing happens."[4] God is the healer. "Faith reaches out to God and expects and receives with thanksgiving whatever God gives but does not produce or control what is given."[5] Our faith does not control the healing of God, but our faith serves as an instrument through which God may choose to work to provide healing for patients, as well as ourselves. "Praying for healing is a bold act."[6] Social, spiritual, or emotional barriers might arise in our minds: Do I have the authority to pray such a prayer? What will the family think about this prayer? What if nothing happens? Such questions cause us to fear the unknown. It causes us to shrink from praying such prayers. Yet, we are reminded to be people and ministers of faith. We are reminded by the Scriptures to trust God and believe in God's Word. It is not up to us to be healers. That job is squarely in God's hands. Our job is to pray for healing if the patient asks for it. Our job is the comfort the family members, who are dealing with a very difficult situation and the possibility of the loss of their loved one. Our job is not to second-guess what God is going to do. Our job is to act according to the wisdom that is provided by God. Our job is to trust God. Our job is to trust God's Word. We are not responsible for the outcome. Only God knows and is responsible for the outcome. God will provide the healing and wholeness as He wills. We are called to be instruments of faith—faith in God and faith in His Word.

Prior to praying for healing for an individual, one should pray for discernment. The following process is recommended:

1. Invite God to use you as a channel of healing and to continue to give you whatever faith, discernment, and love is necessary to help the person you are praying for.

2. Ask God to melt away anything in you that might get in the way: your need for power, your hang-ups or judgment, your brokenness, or your desire

Ministering Healing and Wholeness to the Dying

to cling to your own agenda. Know that God is able to use you despite these things.

3. Feel your love and compassion for the person. Sometimes this is even more important than faith. Your own love for the person will probably carry with it your human desire for the person. Your instinct may be to say, for example, " I want this person to be healed, physically."

4. Speak your desire to God as honestly and plainly as you can. Put your agenda in God's hands.

5. Then, in silence, ask God how you should pray. Allow your agenda to be changed. Listen for the way God might want to heal this person. Remember, even if a person is eventually healed physically, some other kind of healing may emerge first, for example, the release of anger.

6. After inviting God to shape your agenda, trust God will communicate with you in some way. Pay attention to the images, words that form in your

heart, physical sensations, hunches, intuitions, verses of Scripture that come to mind, and the like. You might try to pray with faith imagination, seeing Jesus with the person (seeing Jesus laying hands on the person—*added by C. V. Hodge*). Remember, God speaks in many ways. It may be easier to trust what you discern when praying with one or more persons rather than alone.

7. Once you sense God speaking in some way, ask yourself, "Does this seem consistent with the character of Jesus?" "Does it sound like the God of the Bible?" "Is it consistent with the best we know of theology and psychology?" "Does it echo the wisdom of the church?" For example, discernment that suggests God is using illness and pain to punish someone for his or her sins is very questionable indeed, because it does not meet the criteria of love and compassion.

8. Proceed with your prayer, humbly using whatever discernment you were given. Act in faith, holding open the possibility that your discernment is

incomplete or even inaccurate. Continue discerning each time you pray.[7]

If you discern the person for whom you are about to pray as smiling and healthy, then you might consider praying, "Lord, please restore this your beloved to full health so that he/she might walk in joy with you." If you discern a sadness, then you might consider praying, "Lord, please reveal any deep sadness that this your loved one may have. Please uncover it so that we may pray aright. Please enter into this sadness by Your Holy Presence to heal the cause thereof." If you discern the word "rest," then you might wish to pray that God grant the individual the rest that he/she needs as he/she is comforted by Your Presence. These are just a few examples of healing prayers that could be considered.

Keep in mind that prayers for the sick can take place without the sick person being present. However, it is good to be face-to-face with the one needing the prayer, because that individual can help with the discernment process. The individual may even provide first-hand information about their condition, as well as their desire for a specific prayer. Remember, we are there to serve and be of assistance to them and their needs, not our own. In addition, being face-to-face with the ill person gives us an opportunity to provide the human touch, whether it is the laying-on-of-hands or the anointing with oil or the serving of the Eucharist. Sometimes they need a hug or a hand held. These are ways God reflects and transmits His love for that person. Be as sensitive and respectful to the person as possible.

"The following guidelines are for those who find themselves in [the] pastoring role:

1. Listen to the person who has sought healing. Let him or her know you are listening by putting the person's feelings in your own words. This can be part of the prayer itself or a brief comment you make before you pray. For example, a person may have had a cancer biopsy but does not yet have the results. Your response might be, "You sound so worried and scared." This sounds easy, but it takes lots of practice to do well. Friends can

practice verbalizing feelings by listening to stories of each other's lives.

2. Listen to God. Pay attention to whatever discernment may come to you even as the person speaks.

3. Do not give advice. You just might be wrong. Even if you are right, you risk making the person dependent on you.

4. Do not say, "I know just how you feel," even if you have been through a similar experience. Remember that each person's response is unique, and the person you are talking to may have reacted quite differently from you. Even if the difference is subtle, it must be respected.

5. Witness to your own faith as you feel led, but from an "I" position. Saying, "Don't you know that God loves you?" may make a sick person feel guilty and wrong. And saying, "Remember that God loves you," can sound preachy. But if you say, "I believe that God loves you." You are simply bearing witness to your own faith.

6. Allow the person to cry. Let yourself relax in the presence of tears. Often gentle tears are the lubrication of God's action in a person. Provide tissues, and let the Lord work.

7. As you pray with another, be comfortable with periods of silence. You do not have to think up beautiful words. The words you do say can be very simple. Trust that the Holy Spirit prays through you *"with signs too deep for words"* (Romans 8:26) and will give you whatever words you need.

8. When it seems helpful to pray for a person using soaking prayer, you may run out of words very quickly. Then you can just sit in God's presence with your hands on the person, trusting God to be at work. During soaking prayer you can visualize or otherwise imagine the person with Jesus. Watch what Jesus does; listen to what He says. Pay attention to emotions he seems to show. You might want to ask the person for whom you are praying to invite Jesus into his or her imagination.

9. Before you finish the prayer time, thank God for hearing you and for being at work in the person. In faith, ask God to continue the healing process.[8]

After praying for the person, let go and let God continue to do His work for that person. It is suggested that you do the letting go as follows:

1. As the prayer session ends, release the person prayed for to God's care. Give up any burden you have taken and any need to have the person be made well according to your agenda. Ask God to heal any brokenness in you that has surfaced during the prayer. Then let God take care of you for a bit. Spend some time resting in God' presence, letting yourself be nourished.

2. Continue to pray for the person regularly, but guard against carrying the person as a burden. Let Jesus do the carrying. Your part is simply to love and pray.

3. Be absolutely trustworthy about keeping confidences. This means no one outside the prayer group should know anything that was said or done during the time of healing prayer. Nothing can destroy a healing ministry faster than to be careless in this respect.

4. Be sure to lighten up. As a healing ministry grows, it becomes increasingly vital to take regular time off for rest—for fun and silliness, for your own growth and creativity, for whatever renews you.[9]

If a family member needs prayer, then pray for them. Ask them if there is something specific that he/she needs. As noted above, seek discernment from God, as well, and then pray accordingly. Sometimes all a person needs is you presence—just being there for him/her. This serves as healing for that person, as well. Some may be healed. Others may not be healed. Although the cure does not manifest itself in the patient, God is still at work in that individual. It is very possible that the individual needs another kind of healing—a healing of past memories, past sins, forgiveness, reconciliation—God may choose to address these needs in lieu of a physical cure. Then, again, God may opt to do both for the person—providing healing and wholeness. We are servants and friends of God. Our only task is to be a vessel for God's purpose. We are not responsible for the healing and wholeness of the person, God is. Keep in mind; you can be healed even when you are not cured. More discussion about this will follow.

Even though mom succumbed to her illness, I believe that God met her need. She was at peace with whatever the outcome was for her. She experienced wholeness in that she was comforted by God's presence in her life, by God's Word as revealed in the Bible, and by the readings that she read. The doctors did all that they could do physically. The nurses eased her suffering through the administering of medications. In the end, God delivered her from her illness. He protected her from any further pain and suffering. He caused her to rest from this trial. She was healed spiritually and she was made whole.

There are many stories of healing (curing) in the Scriptures with which we are all very familiar. Also, there are many stories of healing that I have witnessed and experienced. For example, God healed a very dear friend of our family. This was an elderly woman in her eighties. She was suffering with pneumonia when she was admitted to the hospital. She had a history of heart disorder; however, she had never experienced a heart attack. She was fully grounded in her Christian faith. She lived alone and was doing very well, physically, before the onset of the pneumonia. She was admitted to the hospital and was placed in Intensive Care. Her doctor had told the family, in essence, that there was very little hope for her survival. Her temperature was extremely high and it appeared that she was succumbing to her illness. Her daughter refused to allow the doctor to take her mother off life support. Her daughter was also very well grounded in her Christian faith. She called on the "elders" of the church, along with other family and friends, to pray for her mother. She and a group of people, including some of the hospital nurses, surrounded the bed of her mother to pray. Within twenty-four hours of that prayer, the elderly woman's vital signs were greatly improved. Within a matter of a few days she was fully recovered. God had healed (cured) her. She was made whole. To this day, she continues to live independently and in good health.

God chooses when, where, why, who, and how He will heal and make whole. We are not asked to judge it. We are asked only to serve God and His creation—His people. We are called to go and do the works that God has placed into our hands to do. We are to minister to His people. God heals and makes whole.

Chapter 7

Ministering Healing and Wholeness To Those Persons Who Experience Spousal Abuse

For the Lord, the God of Israel says: I hate divorce and marital separation (Malachi 2:16a AMP).

This particular Scripture has caused many churches to sweep the issue of domestic violence under the rug, or to minimize the seriousness of this issue. When a victim of domestic abuse comes to the church to seek counseling or some form of help, the victim is made to feel as if he or she is at fault or the cause of the domestic abuse. Quite often, the Scripture noted above is given to the victim to say that God would not approve of any form of separation or divorce. The victim is left with the notion that he or she has to return to the situation and do whatever it takes to reduce the violence in the home.

Domestic violence is a real issue, a very serious issue, and it needs to be dealt with in the church forthrightly. Quite often, the church has seen this issue as "just a marital problem" or "just a family argument." Domestic violence goes well beyond the confines of a marital problem or a family argument. This issue impacts spouses both psychologically, as well as physically. The victims of domestic violence may require long-term counseling. Professionals, who have been educated fully in this area, should be sought out by the church to provide such counseling. This should not be the job of a layperson, who has received rudimentary training in this area. Churches would do well not to attempt to cover up this issue. This is an issue that requires attention. This is not an issue that needs platitudes or random Scripture, but action. This is an issue that requires assistance to the victim—assistance that does not blame the victim for their situation. And if the abuser is a member of the church body, then that individual needs counseling that is direct—counseling that will have a direct impact upon this individual that will cause the violence to cease.

Domestic Abuse and Violence Defined

Domestic violence is defined as "abuse from a current or former intimate partner—boyfriend, ex-boyfriend, husband, ex-husband, girlfriend, ex-girlfriend, wife, ex-wife. Domestic violence can mean physical abuse—pushing, slapping, hitting, or choking. But it also includes such things as:

- **Emotional abuse:** Name-calling, playing mind games, put-downs.

- **Threats:** Can be of physical or emotional harm, to take the children.

- **Intimidation:** Using looks, smashing things, loud voices or actions to put you in fear of what might happen.

- **Isolation:** Controlling where you go, what you do, who you see; driving away friends and family.

- **Sexual abuse:** Forcing you to do sexual acts against your will, physically attacking sexual parts of the body.

- **Economic abuse:** Controlling how the money is spent, taking your paycheck away, refusing to give you money for your needs.

- **Using the children:** Making you feel guilty about the children, using custody or visitation to harass you.

- **Using "male privilege:"** Rigid views of roles and duties of men and women, expecting certain things 'because I'm the man.'"[1]

Data Concerning Domestic Violence

The following statistics concerning domestic violence serve as a reality check for those of us in ministry:

- Battering is the single major cause of injury to women—more frequent than automobile accidents, muggings, and rapes combined (U.S. Surgeon General, 1984).

- As many as 15 million adult women have been victims of battering, rape, and other forms of physical and sexual assault (Crime Victims Digest, 1989).

- Each year, a million or more women are added to the total listed above for battering and other forms of violence (Crime Victims Digest, 1989).

- The recidivism rate for men who have had treatment for abusing their wives ranges from 30% to 40% (Saunders, 1988).

Most domestic violence refers to rape, robbery, aggravated assault, or simple assault committed against a married, divorced, or separated woman by a relative or other person well known to the victim (U.S. Department of Justice, 1986). Contrary to popular belief and current myths, family violence cuts across all racial and economic lines. Victims come from all types of homes. Domestic violence has cut into the fabric of our community and touches the lives of people of all ages and diverse occupations and professions (U.S. Attorney General's Task Force on Family Violence, 1984). The major difference in family violence from other categories of violence is the relationship between the victim and the assailant.

Violence that is committed against a stranger is considered to be an assault. When violence is committed against a family member it is considered a family argument. Violence against a stranger usually ends in an arrest and the perpetrator is charged with assault and battery. Participants in family violence are told to "cool down" (U.S. Attorney General, 1984).[2]

I find it interesting that many victims, who have sought assistance and counseling from their churches, have had the above noted Scripture presented to them. For example, if a victim says to the pastor or the individual assigned by the church to handle such matters, "I can't take it anymore. I have to get out of this situation," the person assigned quite often quickly says, "Well, you know, 'God hates divorce.'" For some reason, the remaining portion of that Scripture is never presented to the victim. The full Scripture says, *"For the Lord, the God of Israel, says: I hate divorce and marital separation, and him who covers his garment [his wife] with violence. Therefore keep a watch upon your spirit [that it may be controlled by My Spirit], that you deal not treacherously and faithlessly [with your marriage mate]"* (Malachi 2:16 AMP). Many churches fail to deal with this Scripture in its entirety. Many churches fail to counsel the abuser with the latter portion of this Scripture. Domestic violence is not something that will fade away. Many victims end up dead or in jail, as a result of taking matters into their own hands. Some end up purchasing firearms and shooting their abusers or committing suicide. Many victims feel that there is little to no assistance provided by the church. Many victims feel as if they are on a merry-go-round with this issue. They believe there are no other options for them.

What Can Ministers Do?

One of the first things a minister should do is to be on the lookout for signs of abuse and battering, such as severe mood swings, constant headaches, nightmares, inability to make decision or act on her own, depression, and self-destructive tendencies, to name a few. "Frequent, repeated exposure to the trauma and the amount of control the abuser exerts over the life of the victim often produce a feeling of hopelessness in the victim that can be emotionally paralyzing."[3] If you should see bruises that occur and reoccur, gently ask the individual if everything is alright. Let them know that you are available to talk with them about any difficulties that they may be having. In other words create a friendly environment in which the victim will feel safe in discussing their issues with you. Create an environment where the victim will not be victimized again by accusations of wrong doing on his/her part.

When the victim comes to see you about the problem, be sure to open the counseling session with prayer. Advise the victim that what they tell you will remain in the strictest confidence. (Do not make this the topic of your next sermon.) Then, ask them to share with you their situation. Allow the victim to talk out their problem. Do not be so quick to give an answer or a solution to the problem. Quite often, the victim will need to "ventilate"—get their concerns, fears, and emotions out. Sometimes there will be tears. Be sure to have a box of tissue available. Sometimes they may even show anger. At such times you should remain calm and work at calming the victim. Do not feel rushed to come up with a solution. Use reflective questions to get at the heart of the matter. For example, "I hear you saying ..." or "I understand you to be saying ...." This allows the victim to talk a little more about that aspect of the problem and to clarify any misconceptions. If you do not feel comfortable in providing this type of counseling, then seek professional assistance.

Domestic violence is a matter of power and control of one person over another. The victim often feels stripped of all power over her life. The victim will need assistance in regaining control of her life in order to move forward. There is one thing to remember that should reconciliation begin to occur, "it should be the victim's decision when she feels ready, if ever, to enter into joint counseling with her batterer, not the counselor's or the batterer's."[4]

In some cases, "healing and wholeness" may be in the form of a separation and ultimately a divorce. The healing in this situation is that the victim is no longer victimized by verbal or physical abuse. The wholeness comes when the victim regains a sense of regaining control in her life. Long-term counseling may be necessary to assist the victim in this process. Some victims recover quickly, once they are removed from the environment of abuse. Others may need a bit more time to recover. Domestic violence has a tremendous impact upon the psychological and emotional makeup of the individual. Feelings of lack of self-worth may abound as a result of physical, psychological, and emotional abuse. These feelings may take quite a bit of time to heal. In this, we are called to be patient with the victim and to provide as much support as possible.[5]

Recommended Resources

The following resources are recommended for pastoral care associated with the subject of domestic violence and abuse:

- Clarke, R. L. (1986). *Pastoral Care of Battered Women.* Philadelphia, PA: Westminster Press.

- Gondolf, E. (1985). *Men Who Batter: An Integrated Approach for Stopping Wife Abuse.* Homes Beach. FL: Learning Publications.

- Sonkin, D., & Murphy, M. (1982). *Learning to Live without Violence: A Handbook for Men.* San Francisco: Volcano Press.[6]

Professional Organizations
In the Washington, D.C., Metropolitan Area

The following organizations are available for referrals; i.e., professional help. They will provide names of organizations that provide counseling services near you.

- Clearinghouse on Family Violence Information
  P. O. Box 1182
  Washington, DC 20013
  703-821-2086

- National Coalition Against Domestic Violence
  P. O. Box 34103
  Washington, DC 20043-4203
  202-638-6388

- The National Council on Child Abuse and Family Violence
  1155 Connecticut Ave., NW, Suite 300
  Washington, DC 20036
  800-222-2000

- National Domestic Violence Toll Free Line
  800-333-7230[7]

Domestic violence is a very serious problem that needs the attention of church leaders. If we consider ourselves a "care-giving" community, then we need to provide better care to the victims of domestic abuse. In addition, we need to seek sources and organizations that will assist in rehabilitating the abuser. This is how we provide healing and wholeness in this situation. Healing and wholeness come when parties feel safe—no longer victimized, no longer abused. Healing and wholeness come when individuals regain their self-esteem, regain control in their own lives. I believe our churches can provide better "care" in the process towards healing and wholeness. This only requires our commitment to do so.

Chapter 8

Conclusion

This book has dealt with the issue of healing and wholeness by first looking at the Biblical text associated with healing and wholeness. Next, we took a look at what the great thinkers in our society have thought about this subject and how their thinking has influenced the church. Two cases were identified as real life examples needing healing and wholeness. Recommendations were provided to dealing with each of these scenarios and recommended readings and referrals were provided. Recommendations for handling each of these scenarios by church leadership have been presented.

It is my hope that this book has piqued the interest of church leaders to dig a little deeper in the Scriptural text and dig a little deeper into the recommended resources as we move toward a church environment of healing and wholeness. We have been called to be "doers of the Word." Are we truly up to the task? I believe with God we are. I pray that this book has been a blessing to you.

End Notes

Chapter 2

1. Frank Bartleman, Azusa Street, (New Kensington: 1982), 39.

2. James Strong, The New Strong's Exhaustive Concordance of the Bible, (New York: Thomas Nelson Publishers, 1984), Greek Dictionary of the New Testament, 36.

3. Ibid.

4. James Strong, The New Strong's Exhaustive Concordance of the Bible, (New York: Thomas Nelson Publishers, 1984), Greek Dictionary of the New Testament, 73.

5. Strong, Greek Dictionary of the New Testament, 70.

Chapter 3

1. Morton Kelsey, Healing and Christianity, (Minneapolis: Augsburg Fortress, 1995), 6.

2. Ibid.

3. Ibid, 6-25

4. Ibid.

5. Ibid, 14.

6. Ibid, 12.

7. Ibid, 6-25.

8. Ibid, 18.

9. Ibid.
10. Ibid, 7, 21-25.
11. Ibid, 21.
12. Ibid, 22.
13. Ibid.
14. Ibid
15. Ibid, 24-25.
16. Ibid.
17. Strong's Concordance, Greek Dictionary of the New Testament, 7.
18. George Mallone, Those Controversial Gifts, (Downers Grove: InterVarsity Press, 1983, 14.
19. Ibid, 14, 17, and 19.

Chapter 4

1. Morris Maddocks, The Christian Healing Ministry, (London: SPCK, 1981), 9.
2. Ibid.
3. Ibid.
4. Bruce G. Epperly, God's Touch, (Louisville: West-minster John Knox Press, 2001), 80.
5. Ibid.
6. Ibid, 84.

Chapter 5

1. Frank Bartleman, Azusa Street. (New Kensington: Whitaker House, 1982), 130-146.

2. Simon Doniger, ed, Healing: Human and Divine (Man's Search for Health and Wholeness Through Science, Faith, and Prayer, (New York: Association Press, 1957), 202-203.

Chapter 6

1. Harold G. Keonig, et. al. Handbook of Religion and Health, (New York: Oxford University Press, 2001), 293.

2. Thomas S. Plante and Allen C. Sherman, Faith and Healing (Psychological Perspectives), (New York: The Guilford Press, 2001), 312.

3. D. S. Latimer, Sickness and Healing in the Church, (Oxford: Latimer House, 1981), 45

4. Richard J. Beckman, Praying for Wholeness Healing, (Minneapolis: Augsburg Fortress, 1995), 24.

5. Ibid.

6. Ibid, 25.

7. Tilda Norbert and Robert Webber, Stretch Out Your Hand (Exploring Healing Prayer), (Nashville: Upper Room Books, 1998), 79-81.

8. Ibid, 84-85.

9. Ibid, 87-88.

Chapter 7

1. Interact of Wake County, NC: Providing Safety and Support, Domestic Violence Defined (Internet)

2. Sandra L. Brown, Counseling Victims of Violence, (Alexandria: American Counseling Association, 1991), 101-102.

3. Ibid, 106.

4. Ibid, 110

5. Note: The majority of these recommendations come from my experience in the Federal workforce. I have over 25 years of training and service in the area of counseling employees. Domestic violence plays out in the workforce, as well as in the church.

6. Brown, 114

7. Ibid.

Bibliography

Allister, D. S. *Sickness and Healing In The Church*. Oxford: Latimer House, 1981.

Bartleman, Frank. *Azusa Street*. New Kensington: Whitaker House, 1982.

Beckman, Richard J. *Praying for Wholeness and Healing*. Minneapolis: Augsburg Fortress, 1995.

Beckman, Sandra L. *Counseling Victims of Violence*. Alexandria: American Counseling Association, 1991.

Howard Clinebell. *Basic Types of Pastoral Care & Counseling (Resources for the Ministry of Healing & Growth)*. Nashville: Abingdon Press, 1966 and 1984.

de Villiers, Pieter G. R. ed. *Healing in the Name of God*. Pretoria: University of South Africa, C. B. Powell Bible Center, 1986.

Doniger, Simon, ed. *Healing: Human and Divine*. New York: Association Press, 1957.

Dossey, Larry. *Healing Words*. New York: Harper Paperbacks, 1993.

Epperly, Bruce G. *God's Touch*. Louisville: Westminster John Knox Press, 2001.

Epperly, Bruce G. *The Power of Affirmative Faith*. St. Louis: Chalice Press, 2001.

Ervin, Howard M. *Healing: Sign of the Kingdom*. Peabody: Hendrickson Publishers, 2002.

Fox, A. H. Purcell. *The Church's Ministry of Healing*. London: The Camelot Press, 1959.

Gordon, A. J. *The Ministry of Healing (Miracles of Cure in All Ages)*. Brooklyn: Christian Alliance Publishing, 1982.

Granbert-Michaelson, Karin. *Healing Community*. Geneva: WCC Publications, 1991.

Kelsey, Morton T. *Healing and Christianity*. Minneapolis: Augsburg Fortress, 1995.

Koenig, Harold G. *Handbook on Religion and Health*. Oxford: University Press, 2001.

Koenig, Harold G. *The Healing Power of Faith*. New York: Simon and Schuster, 1999.

Maddocks, Morris. *The Christian Healing Ministry*. 3d ed. London: SPCK, 1995

Mallone, George. *Those Controversial Gifts*. Downers Grove; InterVarsity Press, 1983.

Martin, Bernard. *The Healing Ministry in the Church*. Richmond: John Knox Press, 1960 (English translation) and London: Lutterworth Press.

Meeks, Wayne A. ed. (NRSV) *The HarperCollins Study Bible*. London: HarperCollins Publishers, 1989.

Nelson, Susan L. *Healing the Broken Heart*. St. Louis: Chalice Press, 1997.

Norbert, Tilda and Webber, Robert D. *Stretch Out Your Hand (Exploring Healing Prayer)*. Nashville: Upper Room Books, 1998.

Peddie, J. Cameron. *The Forgotten Talent*. London: Oldbourne Book Company, 1961.

Peel, Robert. *Spiritual Healing in a Scientific Age*. San Francisco: Harper & Row Publishers, 1987.
Plante, Thomas G. and Sherman, Allen C. *Faith and Health*. New York: The Guilford Press, 2001.

Sanford, John A. *Healing Body and Soul*. Louisville: Westminster/John Knox Press, 1992.

Sperry, Len. *Ministry and Community*. Colegeville: The Liturgical Press, 2000.

Strong, James. *The New Strong's Exhaustive Concordance of the Bible*. Nashville: Thomas Nelson Publishers, 1984.

The Comparative Study Bible. Grand Rapids: Zondervan Bible Publishers, 1984.

Turner, Max. *The Holy Spirit and Spiritual Gifts*. Peabody: Hendrickson Publishers, 1996.

Turabian, Kate L. *A Manual for Writers of Term Papers, Theses, and Dissertations*. (6th ed.) Chicago: The University of Chicago Press, 1937. (Revised by John Grossman and Alice Bennett, 1993).

Wagner, C. Peter. *How to Have a Healing Ministry in Any Church*. Ventura: Regal Books, 1988.

Wagner, James K. *An Adventure in Healing and Wholeness*. Nashville: Upper Room Books, 1993.

White, Ellen G. *The Ministry of Healing*. Kansas City: Pacific Press Publishing, 1909.

Wigglesworth, Smith. *Wigglesworth on the Anointing*. Springfield: Whitaker House, 1999.

Wilkinson, John. *The Bible and Healing*. Grand Rapids: Wm. B. Eerdmans Publishing, 1998.

About the Author

Dr. Carolyn V. Hodge is a native of the Nation's Capital. Formerly, she was the Director of Equal Employment Opportunity with the Department of Justice, Immigration and Naturalization Service. With a plethora of ministry experience, Dr. Hodge has served as Pulpit Minister; as Associate Pastor; as Assistant Pastor; and currently as Founder and Pastor of "I AM The Living Word Ministries."

Dr. Hodge completed graduate study at Antioch School of Law earning a Master's degree in Equal Opportunity Law. She earned a Master of Divinity degree (receiving the Dean's Top Graduate Award) from Howard University School of Divinity (HUSD). As a result of this exposure, she served as Assistant Chaplain at the National Rehabilitation Hospital in Washington, D.C. She received an Honorary Doctor of Divinity degree; and earned a Doctor of Ministry degree from Wesley Theological Seminary of Washington, D.C. Dr. Hodge was ordained a Reverend in the Pentecostal Discipline and licensed in the D.C. Superior Court in 1999 under the leadership of Rev. Dr. Judy Fisher, Senior Pastor of the Church of the Lords Missions International of Washington, D.C.

www.ingramcontent.com/pod-product-compliance
Lightning Source LLC
Chambersburg PA
CBHW072058290426
44110CB00014B/1731